MY FIRST
FAMILY TREE
BOOK

By Catherine Bruzzone
Illustrated by Caroline Church

Ideals Children's Books • Nashville, Tennessee
an imprint of Hambleton-Hill Publishing, Inc.

Published by Ideals Children's Books
An imprint of Hambleton-Hill Publishing, Inc.
Nashville, Tennessee 37218

First published in Great Britain
by b small publishing for The Early Learning Centre
Swindon, England

Copyright © 1991 by b small publishing

Printed in Hong Kong.

ISBN 0-8249-8546-X

A family tree

Your family tree shows how you are related, or connected, to other people in
your family—just like a tree's branches are connected to the tree trunk. On the
opposite page, a simple family tree is shown. Look at the lines connecting you to
your sister and brother, mother and father, and grandmothers and
grandfathers. These lines show how you are related to your relatives.

This family tree may not look exactly like your family—you may have more
brothers or sisters, and you may have aunts, uncles, and lots of cousins. Family
trees can show all these people. They can also give other interesting
facts, such as when your mother was born, how many sisters your
grandmother had, and how old your great-grandfather was
when he died.

You will be able to draw your own family tree at the end of
this book. But before you do, discover as much as you can
about your family as you go through *My First Family Tree Book.*

What to do if you find more information than will fit into this book:

If you find more information than will fit into this
book, paper-clip extra pages to the book's pages,
or make a special envelope out of the back cover.
1. Cut out a
cardboard
triangle. **2.** Tape
triangle securely
to bottom back
cover corner.
Now you can
insert extra pages into your envelope!

2.

Another option is to make a separate book with
extra pages. First, place pages in order.
Then punch holes
through their left
margins and
thread
string
through the holes.
Tie the ends together
securely in a knot or bow,
and your separate book is ready!

1.

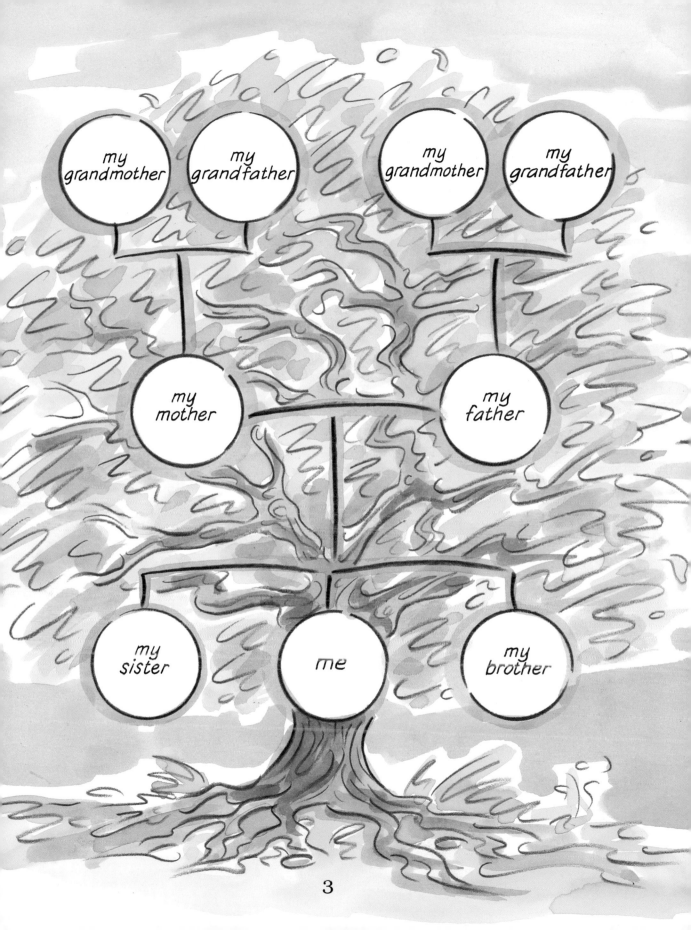

All about me

Date I was born _____

Time I was born _____

Place I was born _____

Ask if you can see your birth certificate. Did someone keep a record when you were a baby?

Weight at birth _____

Length at birth _____

Eye color _____

Hair color _____

Mother's name _____

Father's name _____

Brothers' names _____
_____

Sisters' names _____
_____

Caregiver's name _____

STICK IN
PHOTOGRAPH

me, as a baby

STICK IN
PHOTOGRAPH

me, age _____

4

My name is

Other people I live with

My address

Languages I speak

Names of schools

My phone number

Fill this space with more about yourself or draw a self-portrait

5

My mother

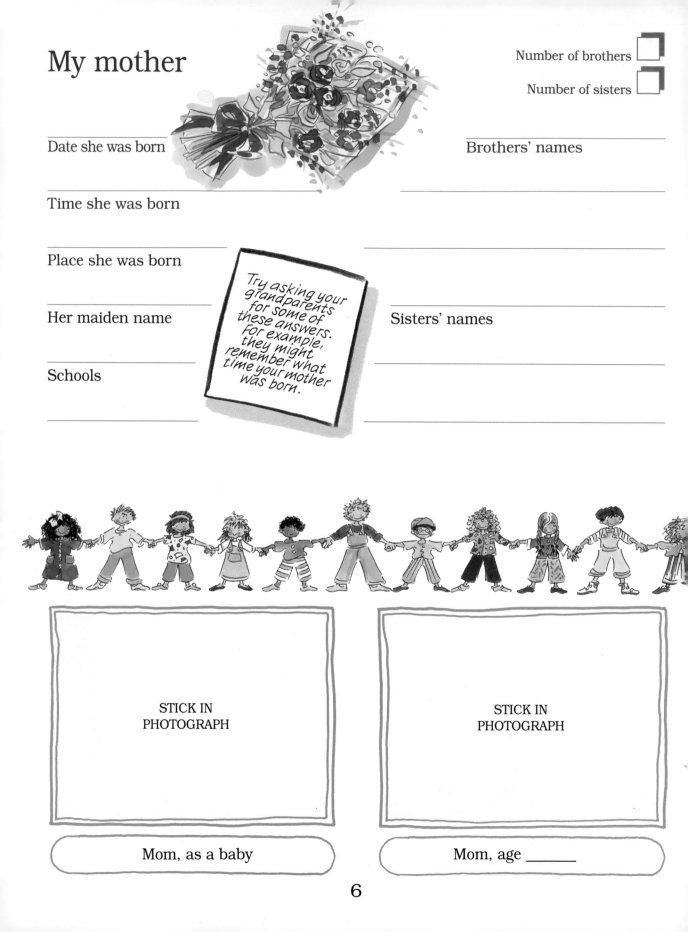

Date she was born

Time she was born

Place she was born

Her maiden name

Schools

Brothers' names

Sisters' names

Try asking your grandparents for some of these answers. For example, they might remember what time your mother was born.

STICK IN
PHOTOGRAPH

STICK IN
PHOTOGRAPH

Mom, as a baby

Mom, age _____

6

Her name is

Diplomas

Can you find your mother's school or college certificates? Did she do swimming, dancing or gymnastics?

Hair color

Eye color

Favorites

Jobs

Her age when I was born

Draw your mother here

My father

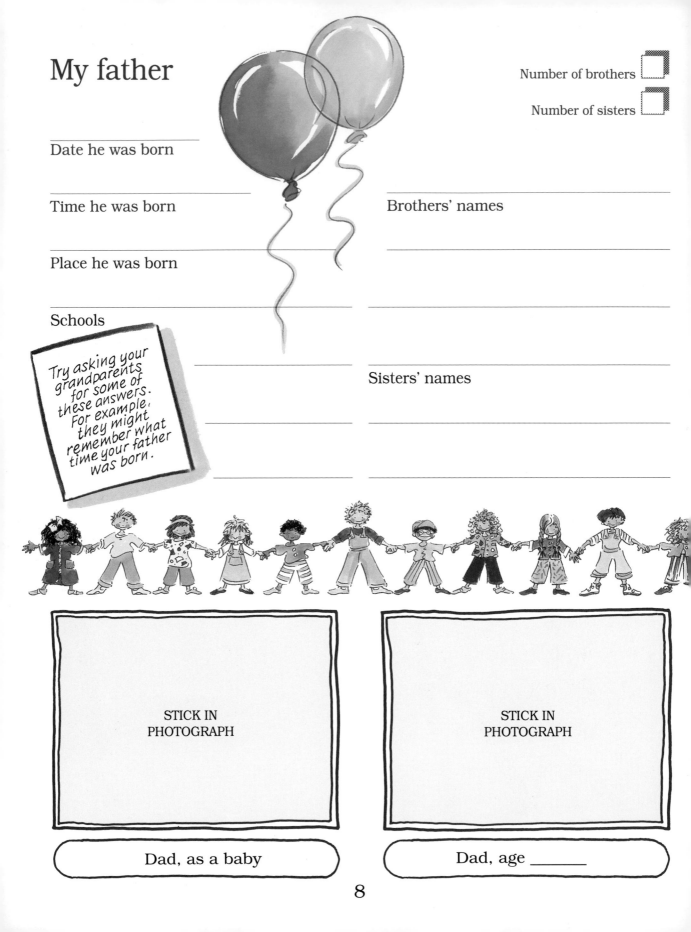

Number of brothers ☐☐

Number of sisters ☐☐

Date he was born

Time he was born

Place he was born

Schools

Brothers' names

Sisters' names

Try asking your grandparents for some of these answers. For example, they might remember what time your father was born.

STICK IN PHOTOGRAPH

Dad, as a baby

STICK IN PHOTOGRAPH

Dad, age _____

His name is

Diplomas

Hair color

Eye color

Jobs

Favorites

His age when I was born

Fill this space with more about your father, or draw a picture of him

My sisters and brothers

Number of brothers ☐

Number of sisters ☐

My oldest sister or brother's name
_____

Date and place he or she was born
_____

Favorites
_____

My next oldest sister or brother's name
_____

Date and place he or she was born
_____

Favorites
_____

My next oldest sister or brother's name
_____

Date and place he or she was born
_____

Favorites
_____

If you have more than 3 sisters and brothers, write their details on a piece of paper and clip it to this page. You can also give details of half-sisters and brothers or stepsisters and brothers.

If you want, say how they are related to you: "Rose is my half-sister. She and I have the same father."

"Robert is my stepbrother. He is John's son. John lives with my mother."

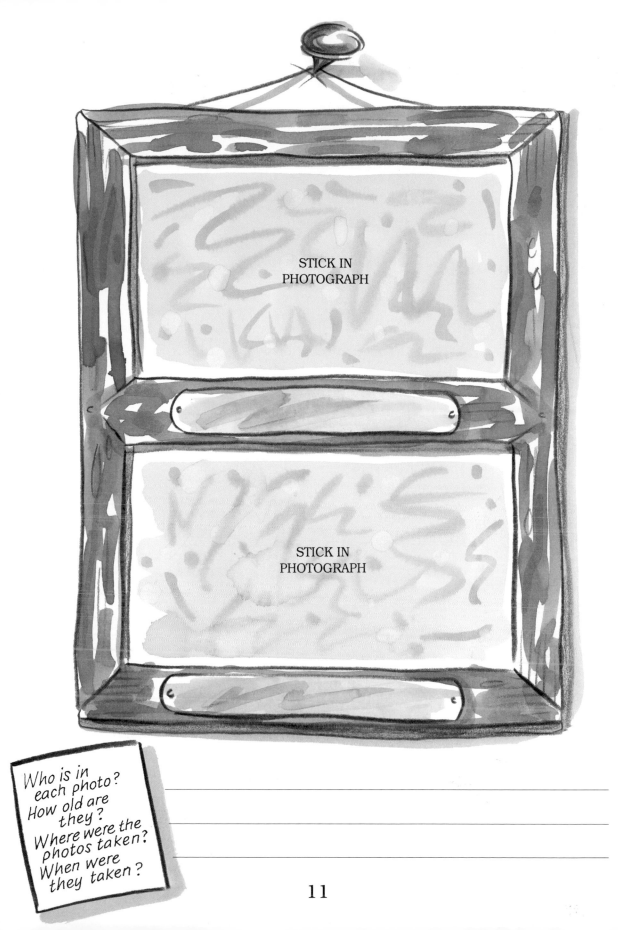

STICK IN
PHOTOGRAPH

STICK IN
PHOTOGRAPH

Who is in each photo?
How old are they?
Where were the photos taken?
When were they taken?

My aunts and uncles

These are my **mother's** sisters and brothers.

My oldest aunt or uncle

My next oldest aunt or uncle

Date he or she was born

Date he or she was born

Place he or she was born

Place he or she was born

Where he or she lives

Where he or she lives

Person he or she lives with

Person he or she lives with

Names of children

Names of children

Your aunts' or uncles' children are your **cousins**. You can fill in more details about them on pages 16 and 17.

My next oldest aunt or uncle

Names of children

Date he or she was born

Place he or she was born

Where he or she lives

If your mother has more than 3 sisters and brothers, write their details on a piece of paper and clip it here. Can you find a photo of your mother and her brothers and sisters as children?

Person he or she lives with

STICK IN
PHOTOGRAPH

STICK IN
PHOTOGRAPH

Write the names of the people in each photo. Where were the photos taken? When were they taken? Do you have a photo of the same people now?

My aunts and uncles

These are my **father's** sisters and brothers.

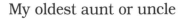

My oldest aunt or uncle

_____

Date he or she was born

_____

Place he or she was born

_____

Where he or she lives

_____

Person he or she lives with

_____

Names of children

_____

_____

_____

_____

My next oldest aunt or uncle

_____

Date he or she was born

_____

Place he or she was born

_____

Where he or she lives

_____

Person he or she lives with

_____

Names of children

_____

_____

_____

_____

Do you have any **COUSINS**? These are your aunts' and uncles' children. Fill in their details on pages 16 and 17.

My next oldest aunt or uncle

_____

Date he or she was born

_____

Place he or she was born

_____

Where he or she lives

_____

Person he or she lives with

Names of children

_____

_____

_____

_____

See if you can find a photo of your father and his brothers and sisters as children.

STICK IN
PHOTOGRAPH

STICK IN
PHOTOGRAPH

_____

_____

Write the names of the people in each photo. Where and when were the photos taken? Do you have a photo of some of the people now?

My cousins on my **mother's** side

These are my **mother's** nieces and nephews.

If your parents come from a large family, you may have lots of cousins! Start on your mother's side. First put her oldest brother or sister's name and then fill in the details for each cousin.

Their parents' names

Their parents' names

Name of oldest child

Name of oldest child

Date and place he or she was born

Date and place he or she was born

Name of next oldest child

Name of next oldest child

Date and place he or she was born

Date and place he or she was born

Name of next oldest child

Name of next oldest child

Date and place he or she was born

Date and place he or she was born

My cousins on my **father's** side

These are my **father's** nieces and nephews.

Paste a photo of your cousins on a sheet of paper. Under it, write their names and how old they are.

Their parents' names
_____

Name of oldest child
_____

Date and place he or she was born
_____

Name of next oldest child
_____

Date and place he or she was born
_____

Name of next oldest child
_____

Date and place he or she was born

Their parents' names
_____

Name of oldest child
_____

Date and place he or she was born
_____

Name of next oldest child
_____

Date and place he or she was born
_____

Name of next oldest child
_____

Date and place he or she was born

If you don't have a photo of your cousins, draw a picture of them. Which of your cousins is the tallest and which is the smallest?

My grandmother

This is my **mother's** mother.

If your grand-parents are no longer alive, you may need to do some detective work to fill in these pages. Can your mother and father help? Or your aunts and uncles?

_____
Her name

_____
Name I call her

_____
Her maiden name

_____
Date and place she was born

_____
Her brothers' names

_____
Her sisters' names

_____
Schools

_____
Jobs

_____
Date and place of her wedding

_____
Her age when my mother was born

_____
Something she remembers

_____

_____

STICK IN
PHOTOGRAPH

My grandmother, age _____

18

My grandfather

This is my **mother's** father.

His name _____

Name I call him _____

Date and place he was born _____

His brothers' names _____

_____

His sisters' names _____

_____

Schools _____

_____

Jobs _____

_____

His age when my mother was born _____

Something he remembers _____

_____

_____

_____

_____

STICK IN
PHOTOGRAPH

My grandfather, age _____

Ask about the things that were different when your grandparents were young. What style of clothes did they wear? What games did they play? Can they remember something important in the news? Why not make a book or a cassette recording of their memories?

19

My grandmother

This is my **father's** mother.

Her name _____

Name I call her _____

Her maiden name _____

Date and place she was born _____

Her brothers' names _____

_____

Her sisters' names _____

_____

Schools _____

_____

Jobs _____

_____

Date and place of her wedding _____

Her age when my father was born _____

Something she remembers _____

_____

_____

STICK IN
PHOTOGRAPH

My grandmother, age _____

Look at the notes on pages 18 and 19

20

My grandfather

This is my **father's** father.

His name _____

Name I call him _____

Date and place he was born _____

His brothers' names _____

_____

His sisters' names _____

_____

Schools _____

Schools _____

Jobs _____

His age when my father was born _____

Something he remembers _____

_____

_____

STICK IN
PHOTOGRAPH

My grandfather, age _____

Can someone show you your grandparents' marriage certificate? It will tell you when and where they were married.

21

My own family tree

On a separate sheet of paper, make a simple family tree using page 3 as a guide. Include just your grandparents, parents, and brothers and sisters, placing your eldest brothers and sisters on the left and the youngest on the right.

Ask someone to help you make a larger tree showing your aunts, uncles, and cousins, and perhaps your grandparents' brothers and sisters and your great-grandparents.

You could add special details to your tree, such as those shown below. Once you are satisfied with the appearance of your family tree, carefully copy it on the space provided here.

Granny Black
b. 1 June 1923
Swansea

b. = born
m. = married
d. = died

Discovering more about your family

Letters: family news, events, celebrations

Photograph albums: physical similarities between relatives, clothing tastes

Postcards: information on travels

Family Bibles: dates of weddings, births, and deaths

Diaries: family members' thoughts and concerns, similarities in personalities and tastes

Scrapbooks: dates, news, photos, etc.

Baby record books: important event and firsts

Yearbooks: special activities, names of friends

Report cards: school performance, attitudes toward schoolwork and others

Other places you can explore

County clerk's offices: property information, tax records

Libraries: national and state events, styles and fads during specific years

Churches: dates of christenings, confirmations, etc.

Cemeteries: full names, birth and death dates, spouse's names

Newspaper offices: local events on important dates, announcements